RED ZONE

poems by

Beatrice Szymkowiak

Finishing Line Press
Georgetown, Kentucky

RED ZONE

Copyright © 2018 by Beatrice Szymkowiak
ISBN 978-1-63534-750-0 First Edition
All rights reserved under International and Pan-American Copyright Conventions. No part of this book may be reproduced in any manner whatsoever without written permission from the publisher, except in the case of brief quotations embodied in critical articles and reviews.

ACKNOWLEDGMENTS

"To Hold a Grenade" features in the Januaruy 2018 issue of *Borderlands: Texas Poetry Review*.

This chapbook would never have been written without the unconditional love and support of my wife, Nicole E. Taylor. I would also like to thank the [K]nightbreakers and my mentors at the Institute of American Indian Arts: Joan Naviyuk Kane, Santee Frazier, James Thomas Stevens and Sherwin Bitsui for their insightful feedbacks and their continuous support.

Publisher: Leah Maines
Editor: Christen Kincaid
Cover Art: Beatrice Szymkowiak
Author Photo: Nicole E. Taylor
Cover Design: Elizabeth Maines McCleavy

Printed in the USA on acid-free paper.
Order online: www.finishinglinepress.com
 also available on amazon.com

Author inquiries and mail orders:
Finishing Line Press
P. O. Box 1626
Georgetown, Kentucky 40324
U. S. A.

Table of Contents

To Hold a Grenade 1

The Angel's Share 2

Vimy, WWI Canadian Memorial and Battlefield, France 3

The Unknown Soldier 4

Where Trenches Were 5

Phosgene 6

Afterschool Children Would Play Sarbacane in the

    Small Wood Behind the House 7

Madonna of the Pomegranate 8

Flanders Fields: Summer Solstice 9

What Prevails 10

[Fleury-Devant-Douaumont:] 11

CODA 25

Maryhill Stonehenge WWI Memorial, WA 26

Notes 27

"The environment destruction left by the battle led to the creation of the Zone Rouge—the Red Zone."

To Hold a Grenade

hold grenade
       well   hold ground
                up toward primer   flickering leaf light

    contained

so as to grow
       downward
               hold radicles
                     lever firmly in position

do not remove pin
      plumule
             hold
                until just before
                until roots
                until upward
                until
                      throwing grenade

after removing pin
              keep eyes *hand closed*
                but not clenched
                so as to peel off
                         outer shell
      effort necessary
              to hold lever down
              to hold on
              to an oak
                    is slight, but must be
continuous
      while seedlings
              hold
                    grenade is set
        at "ready"
              and sun particles

The Angel's Share

crushed grape clusters. yield wild yeasts. ferment. sour must. glides along swan's neck. drips. eau-de-vie. into copper. still. double-burnt spirit. ambers. inside oak. barrels blackening walls. sealed gold hour glass. wicker-wrapped carboy. the *bonbonne* was buried. in a cabbage patch. before the bombs.

Vimy   WWI Canadian Memorial and Battlefield, France.

among scatters   of young trees
                                                                                    not yet felled
       sheep lick dew
                                  above taut silence
graze
       morning clearing
                              grass
beyond danger
                    no entry non-
                                exploded explosives
mingled bone shrapnel   who
                                            is who
       grows into pasture
                              lamb bearing
ewes feed on
                    before crows burst

The Unknown Soldier

his cleaved breast
    bone rises blue

                                        metal-colored flames
                  lead soldiers   he & his dad

melt into bullets
    four bonded hands

                      a corroded pan   Dad's
                                        callous palms

my dirt-covered fingers
    from fallow fields

                              children glean metal
                        scraps or pebbles

weld blue sky
    into leaden seeds

Where Trenches Were

in mid summer we dug
rainstorm river beds

with wooden sticks
watched

them overflow
& devoured

to corrugated seed shells
sweet ripe peaches not yet

creased with questions
in our tender sticky hands

Phosgene

All is quiet on the Western front
wheat reaped flour milled   mothers

knead bread for all
the scarecrows hares ignore—

chasing birdshot pellets
to halt their haste

through listless mist   magpies
pluck musty hay   wreathe

nests within mangled willow
clefts where speckled egg

shells hatch obsidian
                         wings & light

After School Children Would Play Sarbacane in the Small Wood Behind the House

    battle burst black   elderberries blown
from brother's cheeks   into brother's throat
      pith pitted wood   gasps for air & ammunition
             we spat   at each other

Madonna of the Pomegranate
Sandro Botticelli

Granada's garden exceedingly
red seeded apple propagates

alms to sons
who will bloom
sanguine arils

from hand grenade
to incarnadine bloodshot blossom

Flanders Fields: Summer Solstice
for John McCrae

sun fields
              burst
gravel & tar
      sealed eyelids

poppy red
      flakes & black
             powder explode
soldiers in carnival

      skull bones sway
standing still
            wheat threshed light
ebbs

What Prevails

how thick
the fog
down the
furrows plough
shares churn
slow soil &
shrapnel our
lips part
in still-
-ness   yet

                        a murmuration of starlings

[Fleury-Devant-Douaumont:]
  [Village Détruit-Zerstörtes Dorf-Destroyed Village:]

            unruffled forest
                  from forestis silva: outside wood
                        from foris: outside
                                    out of doors

   [interdit-verboten-forbidden:]

                red zone

                        —great grand father
                            from the porch
                                staring   *mute*

[mairie-rathaus-town hall:]

12 million unexploded shells
                approximations rust
                                betweenroots

—father his brothers playing in fields
                            in woods
                            in makeshift
                                    forts

                bat colonies roost in overgrown ruins
                                        rustle dusk
                    with restless darts

[tisserand-weber-weaver:]

                in suspended wings
        broad leaves and needles
                                seep mist
                                        seconds elongated
                                                onto moist soil

                corroding underground
                                shells leak
                                        chlorinephosgene
        fluid countdown

                                —mother young phalanges
                                        glean dirt-covered potatoes
                                                or rusty grenades

[cantonnier-strassenarbeiter-road mender:]

    only light boars
               badgers foxes
                        thread their way through
  undetonated undergrowth

                            shrapnelspades spectaclesgoodluck
                                          horseshoes
                          oxidizetobarbed wire

                                              —born &

[exploitation agricole-bauernhof-farm:]

—my brothers I iron harvests

                                        80,000 deadmenbodies
                                                      or so
                                    rot labyrinthine
                                            skeletons inboots

                                  among planted pine
                                          gnarled pear limbs bear
                                                              soldier fruit
                        offshoots

[café épicerie-lebensmittel-café grocery:]

    craters trenches abound
                buttonsbadgesbullets perforated bowls
        16 inch bent bladebayonets
              arsenic

                      —naming the wood
                              outside

    yellow-bellied toads frogs salamanders
        crested newts thrive in countless
                    phosphorescent pond

[maréchal ferrant-hufschmied-blacksmith:]

         horsesdogs pigeons donkeysnameless
                              corpses tuber
                                      into russets

     kentucky blue-eyed grass
            fallen from army horse
                      hooves bloom in clearing

                                        —before it disappears

CODA

Maryhill Stonehenge WWI Memorial, WA

on the hilltop wind turbines
        grind languid air into sparks

overlooking the colossal river

hanging stone
        reinforced concrete replica

to the memory of […]

ironhorizons
        hidden behind hills

notorious for large destructive
                fast-moving fires

sagebrush and basalt hingedfrombluffs

grapes ripen to wine
        bees pollinate wind

barbwirefencerusts

the altar stone aligned
        with astronomical horizon

or magnetic field

Notes

—In "How to Hold a Grenade," the words in italics come from old World War I manuals.

—In "Phosgene," the words in italics are the title of the famous book by Erich Maria Remarque relating the woes of soldiers during World War I.

—The quote at the beginning of the book comes from an article by Thornton Stuart in the May 2014 issue of the *National Geographic*.

Beatrice Szymkowiak was born in the North of France, a landscape scarred by the battles of WWI trench war. She immigrated to the United States in 2003 and lived in New Orleans, where she witnessed the human and environmental catastrophe caused by Hurricane Katrina and the levee failures. After moving with her wife to Portland, OR, she obtained dual French-US citizenship and earned an MFA in Creative Writing from the Institute of American Indian Arts. Exploratory and experimental, her poetry investigates the new environmental trajectory of the anthropocene. *Red Zone* is the first chapter of her investigations, located at the collusion of personal and general histories, land and language, nature and human nature, geological and human scales.

www.ingramcontent.com/pod-product-compliance
Lightning Source LLC
LaVergne TN
LVHW041513070426
835507LV00012B/1535